D0454907

PLAY DIRECTING

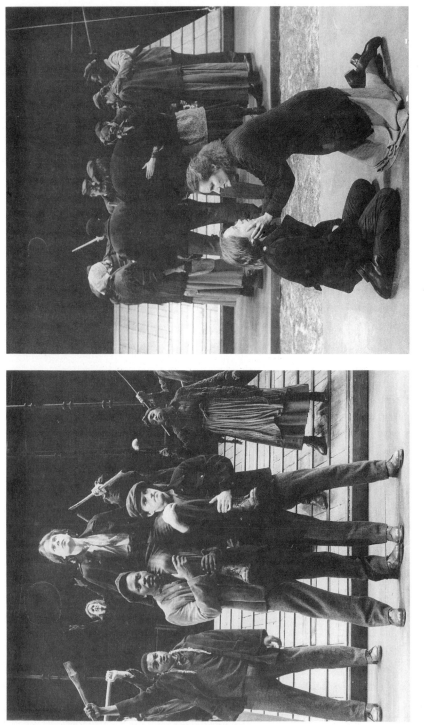

Pulitzer Prize winner, 1992: *The Kentucky Cycle* (Robert Schenkkan); director, Warner Shook; photo, Jay Thompson; from the Mark Taper Forum Production, 1992.

FOURTH EDITION

PLAY DIRECTING
Analysis, Communication, and Style

Francis Hodge
University of Texas

PRENTICE HALL, Englewood Cliffs, New Jersey 07632

Library of Congress Cataloging–in–Publication Data
Hodge, Francis.
    Play directing: analysis, communication, and style / Francis
Hodge.—4th ed.
      p. cm.
    Includes bibliographical references and index.
    ISBN 0-13-501107-8
    1. Theater—Production and direction. I. Title.
  PN2053.H6 1993
  792'.0233—dc20

                                                                    93-1829
                                                                    CIP

Acquisitions editor: Ted Bolen
Editorial/production supervision: Alison D. Gnerre
Cover design: Tommy Boy
Cover photo credit: Gary S. Chapman/Image Bank
Production coordinator: Kelly Behr

Printed in the United States of America

10 9 8 7 6 5 4 3 2

ISBN 0-13-501107-8

Prentice-Hall International (UK) Limited, London
Prentice-Hall of Australia Pty. Limited, Sydney
Prentice-Hall Canada Inc., Toronto
Prentice-Hall Hispanoamericana, S.A., Mexico
Prentice-Hall of India Private Limited, New Delhi
Prentice-Hall of Japan, Inc., Tokyo
Simon & Schuster Asia Pte. Ltd., Singapore
Editora Prentice-Hall do Brasil, Ltda., Rio de Janeiro

CONTENTS

LIST OF PLAYS USED IN PHOTOGRAPHS

LIST OF AUTHORS WHOSE PLAYS APPEAR IN PHOTOGRAPHS

DEDICATION AND CREDITS FOR PHOTOGRAPHS

This edition is dedicated to all those who have helped to keep the speaking theatre alive and well during these years when musical theatre, motion pictures, and television have threatened its existence. Some people say that directing is a job for the young in spirit if not in age, and this I believe, for a play is a poem that needs the lyricism and excesses of youthful spirits if it is to fly with the angels.

I am specifically indebted to the directors and designers who have so generously contributed the many photographs of productions used throughout the book to play "The Game of Visual Perception" (see Chapter 4 for a full explanation). Without their help I could not have assembled this "game" with such variety in choice of plays, and with directors from so many areas and levels of live theatre production in America.

Each photograph is credited here in the order of its use with the following notation: number of the photograph; title of the play and its author; specific director, designer, photo credits, and, where appropriate, actor credits, and the place of production. I have used as examples of student work those productions with which I am most familiar—those at the University of Texas at Austin.

The following plays were designed and staged by student directors: Photos 2, 6, 7, 8, 9, 11, 22, 33, 46, 65, 68, 71, 74.

> Frontispiece: Pulitzer Prize Winner for 1991: *The Kentucky Cycle* (Robert Schenkkan); director, Warner Shook; photo, Jay Thompson; from the Mark Taper Forum Production, 1992.

1 *School for Scandal* (Richard Brinsley Sheridan); director, Austin Pendleton; sets, Andrew Jackness; lighting, Roger Meeker; costumes, David Murin; photo, Phyllis Belkin; actors, Tom Tammi, Stephen Hough, George Morfogen, James Naughton, Laurie Metcalf, Richard Kneeland, Diane Venora, Patricia Swanson, Stephen Lawson; Williamstown Theatre Festival, Williamstown, Massachusetts.

2 *Misalliance* (George Bernard Shaw); director-designer, Michael McLain; University of Texas at Austin.

3 *The Importance of Being Earnest* (Oscar Wilde); director, Patricia W. Cook; scenery, Bill Sherry; costumes, Jim Swain; lighting, Bob Guthrie; Baylor University.

4   *Oliver!* (Lionel Bart); director, Margaret Elizabeth Becker; scenery, Gerhardt Arceberger; costumes, Karen Hudson; lighting, Alfred Stanley; Zachary Scott Theatre Center, Austin, Texas.

5   *Undiscovered Country* (Arthur Schnitzler, tr. Tom Stoppard); director, Nikos Psacharopoulos; sets, David Jenkins; lighting, Arden Fingerhut; costumes, Jennifer vonMayrhauser; photo, Bob Marshak; Williamstown Theatre Festival, Williamstown, Massachusetts.

6   *The Philanthropist* (Christopher Hampton); director-designer, Peter Chapek; University of Texas at Austin.

7   *Ballad of the Sad Cafe* (Edward Albee); director-designer, Esmer Wear; University of Texas at Austin.

8   *Private Lives* (Noel Coward); director-designer, Liz Stuppi; University of Texas at Austin.

9   *Look Back in Anger* (John Osborne); director-designer, Mark Ramont; University of Texas at Austin.

10   *The Resistible Rise of Arturo Ui* (Bertolt Brecht); director, Heinz-Uwe Haus; University of Kansas.

11   *Rosmersholm* (Henrik Ibsen); director-designer, Lawrence Peters; University of Texas at Austin.

12   *The Pope and the Witch* (Dario Fo); director Richard Seyd; photo, Ken Friedman; American Conservatory Theater.

13   *Crimes of the Heart* (Beth Henley); director, James Thomas; scenery, Ken Kloth; costumes, Debra Billow; Marquette University.

14   *Sunday in the Park with George* (Stephen Sondheim and James Lapine); director, Laird Williamson; photo, Larry Merkle; actors, Jeff Keller, Lawrence Hecht, Alice Lynn, Anne Buelman, Ruth Kobart, Gina Ferrall; American Conservatory Theatre, San Francisco.

15   "Guns Ablazing" (Improvisation); photo, Allison Walker; director, Sally Dorothy Bailey; Bethesda Academy of Performing Arts, Bethesda, Maryland.

16   "Guns Ablazing" (Improvisation); photo, Keith Jenkins; director, Sally Dorothy Bailey; Bethesda Academy of Performing Arts, Bethesda, Maryland.

17   *The Seagull* (Chekhov); director, Michael McLain; scenery, Mark Wendland; costume, Mark Wendland; lighting, Michael Nevitt.

18   *Tales from the Vienna Woods* (Odon von Horvath); director, Mladen Kiselow; photo, Richard Trigg; scenery, Paul Owen; costumes, Marcia Dixcy; lighting, Karl E. Haas; Actors Theatre of Louisville.

19   *Good* (C.P. Taylor); director, John C. Fletcher; scenery, Jeffrey Struckman; costume, Beaver Bauer; actor, William Hurt; American Conservatory Theater.

20   *Richard III* (Shakespeare); director, Wally Chappel; Rep. Theatre of St. Louis.

21   *The Kentucky Cycle* (Robert Schenkkan); director, Warren Shook; photo: Jay Thompson; Mark Taper Forum.

22 *The Hostage* (Brendan Behan); directing and staging, Frank Leupold; University of Texas at Austin.

23 *Measure for Measure* (Shakespeare); director, James Thomas; scenery, Randy Wishmeyer; costumes, Elizabeth Kaler; Florida State University.

24 *Death of a Salesman* (Arthur Miller); director, Donovan Marley; scenery and costumes, Robert Blackman; lighting, Steph Storer; PCPA/ theaterfest, Solvang, California.

25 *Sweeney Todd* (Sondheim); director, Jack Wright; University of Kansas.

26 *The Birthday Party* (Harold Pinter); director, Anthony Taccone; sets, John Bonard Wilson; lighting, Derek Duarte; costumes, Jeffrey Struckman; photo, Ken Friedman; actors, Laurence Ballard, Barbara Oliver; Berkeley Repertory Theatre, Berkeley, California.

27 *Child's Play* (Robert Marasco); director, Richard M. Clark; scenery and lighting, Rodney Smith; costumes, Michael Chetterbock; Loretto Heights College, Denver.

28 *Doctor Faustus* (Marlowe); illus. of open staging; scenery, John Rothgeb; director, Francis Hodge; University of Texas at Austin.

29 *The Resistible Rise of Arturo Ui* (Bertolt Brecht); director: Heinz-Uwe Haus; University of Kansas.

30 *Saint Joan* (Bernard Shaw); scenery, Clayton Karkosh; costumes, Paul Rinehardt; director, Francis Hodge; University of Texas at Austin.

31 *Stuck* (Adele Edling Shank); director, Theodore Shank; setting, Andy Stacklin and Kurt Landisman; lighting, Patty Anne Farrell; sound, Alaguis-Sincerco; photo, Allen Nomura; actors, Sherry Conner Steffens, Francine Lembi; Magic Theatre, San Francisco.

32 *Zara Spook and Other Lures* (Ackermann-Blount); director, Kyle Donnelly; photo, Richard Trigg; scenery, Paul Owen; costumes, Lewis D. Rampino; lighting, Ralph Dressler; Actors Theatre of Louisville.

33 *Caligula* (Albert Camus); director, Robert Graham; costumes, Joe Tips; University of Texas at Austin.

34 *A Piece of My Heart* (Shirley Lauro); director, Allen R. Belknap; scenery, Paul Owen; costumes, Michael Krass; lighting, Karl Haas; Actors Theatre of Louisville.

35 *Indians* (Arthur Kopit); director, Jack Gillum; scenery, Elmer S. Peterson; costumes, Ruth Chase; lighting, John R. Dolphin; The Milwaukee Players, Milwaukee, Wisconsin.

36 *The Divorce Court* (Cervantes); scenery, John Rothgeb; costumes, Paul Reinhardt; director, Francis Hodge; University of Texas at Austin.

37 *Rosencrantz and Guildenstern Are Dead* (Tom Stoppard); director, Robert Graham; designer, Bob Dahlstrom; Freddy Wood Theatre, Vancouver, British Columbia.

38 *Doctor Faustus* (Marlowe); the heavens and upper above; scenery, John Rothgeb; costumes, Paul Reinhardt; director, Francis Hodge; University of Texas at Austin.

39 *The Price* (Arthur Miller); director, Dennis Razze; scenery, Michael Sullivan; lighting, Donald Day; costumes, Gaye Bowen; Zachary Scott Theatre Center, Austin, Texas.

40 *Some Enchanted Evening* (Rodgers and Hammerstein); director, Jack Wright; University of Kansas.

41 *Ghosts* (Ibsen); director, Chris Coleman; scenery, Dex Edwards; costumes, Susan Mickey; Alliance Theatre, Atlanta, Georgia.

42 *Charley's Aunt* (Brandon Thomas); director, Edward Hastings; scenery, Joel Fontaine; costumes, Gerald Howland; lighting, Derek Duarte; American Conservatory Theater.

43 *Tobacco Road* (adaptation by Jack Kirkland); director, Jack Wright; University of Kansas.

44 *Brief Lives* (John Aubrey); director, Ray Fry; photo, Richard Trigg; scenery, Paul Owen; costumes, Hollis Jenkins-Evans; lighting, Karl E. Haas; actor, William McNulty; Actors Theatre of Louisville.

45 *The Collection* (Harold Pinter); director, Michael McLain; scenery, Michael McLain; costumes, Judith Burke; lighting, John Lutterbie; Actors Theatre, Austin, Texas.

46 *Bernada Alba* (Lorca); designer and director, Dinal A. Gravel; University of Texas at Austin.

47 *The Council of Love* (Oskar Panizza); director, Jim Fritzler; setting, Niki Psomas; lighting and costumes, Jim Fritzler; photo, Bill Leissner; Big State Productions, Capitol City Playhouse, Austin, Texas.

48 *The Flowering Peach* (Odets); scenery, John Rothgeb; costumes, Lucy Barton; lighting, Neil Whiting; director, Francis Hodge; University of Texas at Austin.

49 *The Kentucky Cycle* (Robert Schenkkan); director, Warren Shook; photo, Jay Thompson; Mark Taper Forum.

50 *Good* (C.P. Taylor); director, John C. Fletcher; scenery, Jeffrey Struckman; costumes, Beaver Bauer; actor, William Hurt, American Conservatory Theater.

51 *Saint Joan* (Bernard Shaw); scenery, Clayton Karkosh; costumes, Paul Reinhardt; director, Francis Hodge; University of Texas at Austin.

52 *Lady from the Sea* (Ibsen); scenery, Clayton Karkosh; costumes, Paul Reinhardt; director, Francis Hodge; University of Texas at Austin.

53 *The Wonderful Wizard of Oz* (Polish version, Jan Skotnicki); director, Lewin Goff; scenery, costumes, lighting, Adam Kilian; Plock, Poland.

54 *The Imaginary Invalid* (Molière); director, Gweneth West; scenery, Dana L. Hanson; lighting, Howard Schumsky; costumes, Cristina M. Olivera; technical director, Sterling Shelton; photo, Shary Connella; University of Florida, Gainesville.

55 *The Effect of Gamma Rays on Man-in-the-Moon Marigolds* (Paul Zindel); director, Sally Russell; scenery, Lee Duran; costumes, Eve Bull; lighting, Beki Willis; Gaslight Theatre, Austin, Texas.

56 *The Effect of Gamma Rays on Man-in-the-Moon Marigolds* (Paul Zindel); director, Sally Russell; scenery, Lee Duran, costumes, Eve Bull; lighting, Beki Willis; Gaslight Theatre, Austin, Texas.

57 *Romeo and Juliet* (Shakespeare); director, Paul Meier; University of Kansas.

58 *Tales From the Vienna Woods* (von Horvath); director, Mladen Kiselow; photo, Richard Trigg; scenery, Paul Owen; costumes, Marcia Dixcy; lighting, Karl E. Haas; Actors Theatre of Louisville.

59 *Cowboy Mouth* (Sam Shepard); director; Kim Kovac; scenery, Kim Kovac; costumes, William Pucilovsky; lighting, Jack Halstead; photo, Dennis Deloria; Paradise Island Express and The Independent Theatre Project, Washington, D.C.

60 *Suicide in B^b* (Sam Shepard); 1980; director, Kim Kovac, scenery, Kim Kovac; costumes, William Pucilovsky; lighting, Jack Halstead; photo, Dennis Deloria; Paradise Island Express and The Independent Theatre Project, Washington, D.C.

61 *Summer and Smoke* (Williams); director, James Thomas; scenery, Lyle Miller; costumes, Elizabeth Kaler; Florida State University.

62 *Tobacco Road* (adaptation by Jack Kirkland); director, Jack Wright; University of Kansas.

63 *Delicate Balance* (Edward Albee); director, Michael McLain; scenery and costumes, Michael McLain; lighting, Patrick Moore; Actors Theatre, Austin, Texas.

64 *Evita* (Andrew Lloyd Webber); director, Dennis Razze; scenery, William Winsor; lighting, James McCabe; costumes, Kathleen Janemski; Allentown College, Center Valley, Pennsylvania.

65 *The Creation of the World and Other Business* (Miller); director-designer, Norman Blumensaadt; University of Texas of Austin.

66 *Curse of the Starving Class* (Shepard); director, Michael McLain; University of California at Los Angeles.

67 *Godspell* (Stephen Schwartz); director, Dennis Razze; scenery, Robert Mond; lighting, James McCabe; costumes, Edward Farley; Allentown College, Center Valley, Pennsylvania.

68 *The Adding Machine* (Elmer Rice); director-designer, Ray Keith Pond; University of Texas at Austin.

69 *Hamlet Dreams* (Celina Sky); scenery, Whizz White; costumes, Jane Hiller-Walkowiak; lighting, James Fallon; director, Celina Sky; Salem State Theatre.

70 *Hamlet Dreams* (Celina Sky); scenery, Whizz White; costumes, Jane Hiller-Walkowiak; lighting, James Fallon; director, Celina Sky; Salem State Theatre.

71 *Sticks and Bones* (Rabb); director-designer, Mike Wheeler; University of Texas at Austin.

72 *True West* (Shepard); director, Sally Russell; scenery and lighting, Whitney White; costumes, Douglas Garland; Salem State College.

Preface

The tradition behind this book dates back more than half a century to the 1930s when courses in play production, with emphasis on directing plays, were first made a formal part of college and university curricula. I am especially grateful to Alexander M. Drummond of Cornell University who taught the enormous value of history of the theatre and dramatic criticism to the directing process, and to Walter Stainton, also of Cornell, who taught, as a trained electrical engineer, that the stage was a machine and when manipulated expertly could produce magic for audiences. Later on, I worked as a colleague with Shakespearean director B. Iden Payne and costumer Lucy Barton who not only strongly supported these approaches in their teaching and practice, but also showed how the meaning of theatre lies in strong personal commitment and in a highly developed understanding of all the crafts of the theatre from playwriting and acting to designing and directing. That is the position taken in this book.

Though the basic theory and approach in this fourth edition of *Play Directing* is the same as in the previous three, there are many changes throughout. I have had the opportunity to clarify some points, update examples, and add new introductions. Previous users of this text will notice that the first four chapters in previous editions have been consolidated into two to enable the student to move more quickly into the directing process. It is suggested, however, that the exercises in these two chapters be given specific attention in order to provide a thorough base for moving ahead. The "Game of Visual Perception" played throughout the book has been revised with new photographs from several levels of production. To give greater emphasis to "hearing" a play in production, visual balance and oral tools have been coordinated in one chapter in Communication 2. In Part Three on interpretation, the chapter on "New Plays" has been much expanded to give these plays primary attention in line with recent programming in community and university theatres. The Epilogue has also been updated to show opportunities for directors as reflected in changes in the 1970s and 1980s.

I want to thank especially the many students, both undergraduate and graduate, who helped work out the many exercises that appear throughout the text, and the directors at all levels who helped illustrate it with photographs of their productions. I am also indebted to Beulah Hodge and Joseph North, whose many years as producers in public television helped me clarify the absolute necessity of delineating the live speaking-theatre's essential difference from the electronic forms.

Finally, a note about the use of the masculine pronouns—he, his, him—throughout the text when referring to the director. Just as "director" and "actor" are used nowadays to include both sexes, the pronouns are so used here in lieu of a nonexistent neuter form, or such clumsy words as "one" or "one's." Women have been active in the theatre as directors for over half a century, and as actor-managers for many decades before that. Thus, sexual delineation has no meaning whatever. A director earns the job-title through talent and acquired knowledge of the theatre.

Francis Hodge

Chapter One

WHY THE DIRECTOR?

BACKGROUND

The central focus in this book is on the process of directing plays before live audiences. But it is a great deal more than that. It is also about playwriting and the structure of plays, about acting, and about designing, for these are the crafts that constitute the process of directing. In this study you face the challenge of how to be useful in an art form that has done without the director before this century and can, perhaps, do without him in the future. To understand the full range of the director's job you must have a certain mastery of all the things that make up directing; only then can you move up the ladder towards working independently and creatively. This book is intended to lead you through the process of analysis, make you aware of all the avenues of communication open to you, and then expose you to style in plays and their productions.

This book is also intended for playwrights, actors, and designers, for it is about how they can give their fullest expression in the production of plays from the modern repertoire as well as new plays and those of past ages. Many would-be directors, actors, and designers, in the interest of practicing too early what they have learned of the basics, neglect the last part of this study on interpretation and doing your own creative production. They never venture into the more difficult plays and how such study can contribute to the whole process of theatre making.

As you proceed in this study you will become aware, if you don't know it already, that the director, though he leads others in this artistic journey, did not appear on the theatre scene until late in the nineteenth century, and that he didn't take hold in America until after 1915 when the "new" theatre of that day threw out the machine-made stagings of the old theatre and took a fresh and creative stance in playwriting and the production of plays. Out of this ferment came such American playwrights as Eugene O'Neill along with the art-theatre concept, which established specialist designers in each area of production under the central leadership of a director. Previously, "stage managers" had supervised the jobs of helping actors in their roles and the use of the stage, and arranged with the stage carpenter, also a scene painter, the conventional and limited scenery. The actors usually provided their own dress. But after 1915, in step with the European pattern, the director headed a producing organization as a creative executive who was knowledgeable about all the crafts. The director thus became a "name" in the theatre in his own right because it was out of his vision and feeling that audiences would see plays in a coordinated ensemble with actors moving before an artistically arranged staging. The director had come to stay as the primary theatricalist and to set the pattern in the development of the motion picture.

You should also be aware that, because of this new concept, we live in an age of the ash-pile theatre. Just as primitive societies throw out their totems after using them in rituals because they have lost their magic, we do the same today by throwing out production materials once they have been used, or putting them in storage for future alterations. Ash-piling has thus made theatre much more costly than it once was. But on the positive side it means that every production is freshly conceived and creatively executed. You probably have noticed the same thing happening in rock concerts where those with freshly designed staging and lighting are more visually exciting and more enthralling overall. You will become very conscious of *vision* as the director's principal contribution to production as you move through the various steps of this book, for this is what gives a produced play its special magic. The challenge is clear: How expert will you be in perceiving fresh visions and then carrying them through?

You will also note as you proceed in this study that a director has four drives that guide all his work on a play: a *vision* of the play that can dominate all the aspects of production from acting to staging; a *comprehensive knowledge* of the dynamics of plays—their rises and falls, their louds and softs, their slow beats and their fast ones; *skills in communication* that can help actors and designers give their most creative attention to a play; and a very *strong desire to entertain* audiences by exciting their minds, their hearts, and their spirits.

THE DIRECTOR'S JOB

It is precisely because he has so much power in the theatre that so much is expected of the director. Yet the curious paradox is that, like the playwright, he is not actually seen *on* the stage but only *through* the actors and the physical staging provided by the designers. In contrast, symphony and opera conductors, and even football coaches, have a physical presence. They visibly run the performance, with the obvious capability of directly affecting coordination, rhythm, and mood. But the director's work can be measured only in what happens when the actors and designers work on the audience. In this sense, he is a silent partner, though his work beforehand is anything but silent. To the contrary, the director is a talker, a verbal imagist, for *his primary work is communication*—not directly to the audience but *to actors and designers* who then transmit his ideas and pressures to the audience.

The director, then, is a communicator of the highest order. This function is his job, his only reason for being. A director may have very strong feelings about a playscript, but sensitivity, though it will help, will not define his directing capabilities. Because the transfer of his ideas must be made through the minds and feelings of others, the challenge for a director lies in his talent for touching the magic springs in others with what he so vividly imagines and feels himself.

This challenge is the director's paradox. All artists operate within some balance of their subjective-objective selves, but it is the subjective that customarily dominates. The director is an exception, for he does most of his work on the conscious side of the scale. Herbert Blau in *The Impossible Theatre*, a stimulating and soul-searching study of the director's function, contends that "The director must be a brain." This statement does not mean that the director works only in a coldly objective, intellectual way. What it does mean is that *the director must trust his feelings to react primitively and vigorously to what he helps make on the stage*. As the practicing critic in the theatre, he must constantly bring *what he feels and thinks to the surface* so that he can communicate readily with others. The director must perceive; he must evaluate; he must make a diagnosis; and he must devise remedies. His effectiveness in all these actions will lie precisely in his outside-inside responses, his objective-subjective balance. To accomplish this balance, the learning director must become intensively aware of the structures of plays, of the prevailing theories and the training processes of acting, of the physical use of the stage, and of the visual capabilities of design, for at the base the director is the total designer of a production—the principal "idea man" who matches concrete form with imagined ideas.

As all artists, the director must first be an adventurous spirit eager to cut new paths, and he must be capable of "soaring" on the level of the dramatic poet. Too often he is regarded as only an interpreter of the creative works of others; yet if he cannot reach some of the same heights as those achieved by the poet he is attempting to reveal on the stage, he is not fulfilling his function. At his best, he will soar with the angels; but at the same time he must be an engineer-pilot, a professional who is forever landing and taking off. He knows his plane, his instruments, and his flight plan—the limitations that bind his flight, yet simultaneously make it possible. The stage is a flying machine that must be manipulated with the greatest skill. By knowing the limitations of his art form, he will know which way freedom lies and thus be able to lead others to it. Flight-in-restriction is his goal.

But despite all this high-minded talk, you must never forget that your leading purpose is to entertain—"Make them feel! Make them laugh!" But this can mean dozens of things. Here's the rub: A good director does not make "entertainment" as the end-all, for it is *how* he entertains that matter. A much better phrase than the word "entertain" is "turning on" audiences by getting their *involuntary* attention. This is the sort of attention audiences give despite themselves. It is what you as a director do to members of an audience that makes them sit more on the edge of their seats despite the hold-offs and hang-ups. Never forget that "I've got 'em" is the goal.

In our day, we seem obsessed with violence as entertainment in itself. But what makes good plays is not how people are killed, but why. A shootout with the evil ones destroyed and the virtuous surviving, as we can see any night on television, tells us very little, and it merely arouses fears and prejudices and sometimes violence like that portrayed. Remember, good plays—and there are many more that are bad—are made of different stuff.

You will discover early on how easy it is to entertain, but how difficult it is to make good theatre.

Learning directing, as with any craft, is a process of personal discovery—doing basic things over and over until they become second nature. How long the learning process will take is a matter of your capability in perceiving concepts, in getting the message in a very personal way. A book of this sort cannot make you into a director, for no one can actually teach you how to direct any more than he can teach you how to act. What can be done is to put you, as a dedicated learner, on the tracks that can lead to self-discovery. The artist in you will do the rest. The old saying "Life is short and art is long" is true only because artists have been challenged greatly by the demands of their jobs, and then have gone beyond themselves in making art that survives. If you want to be a director—the artistic leader of others in the theatre—you must learn it all.

The concept of the director in this book, then, is considered to be both a master craftsman in the theatre and the dedicated communicator-leader of all those who work with this art form. To carry out this objective, Part I—Taking a Play Apart—presents a detailed way of examining the structure of a play with the purpose of knowing its insides so well the director will have all sorts of ways to communicate with actors and designers. Part II—Communication—is divided into four sections, with the first two focusing on the physical ways and means a director communicates directly with actors, the third on how the director communicates to audiences through his design function of choosing options in staging available to him, and the fourth on how a director can help audiences receive a play. Part III—Interpretation/Style—again deals with play-analysis, but on an advanced and much more sensitive level, designated as *style analysis.* The approach here is to help the director perceive the inherent *individuality* of each play—its style—and then to help him find his own individual self-expression in producing it—the director's style.

Once you have decided to do a play, it is your play to handle with perception and leadership—or manhandle, mutilate, and destroy, if you don't know your job. It is entirely in your hands to make it sing, dance, talk beautifully, have meaning in every line; to make it vibrate, wiggle, squirm, climb ladders; to make an audience want to stand up and cheer. Be a conductor of your symphony not just one in the band. Don't blame the actors. You lead them, and how a play turns out is not their fault but yours. This is not a job for softies.

EXERCISE

1. Did you notice how "theatre" is spelled here? Back in the nineteenth century, dictionary-maker Noah Webster dumped the word into a general category and gave it an "-er" ending, the ending most American publishers have used ever since. But despite this, those who make theatre, especially in New York, have retained the old spelling because of all its special meanings and historical attachments from its European heritage. "Theatre" is a name that connotes heritage, traditions, conventions, public and private communications, mirror images—both visual and aural—great ideas, memorable characters, perceptive sentiments, live audiences, live actors, and much more.

2. How does live theatre, then, differ from the electronic mediums of television and moving pictures beyond the simple fact that it is live?

3. Compare the experience of a theatre performance with that of a religious ceremony. Can you envision the stage director as a "maker of ceremonies" rather than the customary designation, "coordinator" of an entertainment?

4. Why can the director be described as a ritualist who makes rituals?

5. Why is the live theatre more of a "belonging" than watching television or a movie?

6. Is theatre a social institution?

7. Why do you or anyone else want to direct plays? Although you may be aware of the decreased position given to the theatre in our time because of motion pictures and television, are you fully informed on how the theatre has changed under their strong influences? What effect has the experimentations of the 1960s had on present-day theatre as well as its

audiences? The shift of professional theatre away from the commercialism of New York City's Broadway, now more than a quarter of a century ago, to the regional non-profit theatres, supported strongly by state and federal taxes together with private monies, must be taken into any critical evaluation. New York is still of top importance because of its many competing theatres and its large number of newspaper reviewers looking at the same play and its production, but decentralization has made a new-old context across America that is not unlike the city stock company theatres of the nineteenth century. With decentralization has come not only a divergence of theatre centers of quality and many more jobs for actors and playwrights in a rapidly declining medium, but it has encouraged and even fostered a widespread network of amateur-professional groups throughout America.

Chapter Two

CAPTURING THE WILD BIRD
The Dramatic Poet and the Director's Job

Do you know how to read a play? Most people don't, but go at it as if they were reading a short story or novel. A play is very different because it is all starts and stops, and full of gaps, silences, and only a bare minimum of descriptions. Furthermore, it is all dramatic action. As a reader you must imagine all of those by supplying in your mind's eye what the actors and the staging are doing. And since a play is all written dialogue, if you don't know what that is and how it works, you will be lost, or confused, or what is worse, take it all for granted as if it is as plain as the nose on your face.

That is what *play-analysis* is for: a way of getting inside plays so you don't miss their real guts.

THE POET-PLAYWRIGHT AND THE DIRECTOR

> The poet's eye, in a fine frenzy rolling,
> Doth glance from heaven to earth, from earth to heaven;
> And, as imagination bodies forth
> The forms of things unknown, the poet's pen
> Turns them to shapes, and gives to airy nothing
> A local habitation and a name.
>
> Theseus in *A Midsummer Night's Dream*

A play is like a tropical bird—at once exotic in its song and plumage, half-seen and mystical in its darting flight, and illusive and difficult to capture. Our forebears called the makers of these special stories play*wrights* on the assumption that a play could be made just as other craftsmen could make ships (shipwright) or wheels (wheelwright). His product, to be sure, it is not nearly so concrete, for he is a conscious dream-maker who can, with the appropriate use of basic tools, stir up minds and create imaginative flights in others—the audience.

The peculiar characteristic of the playwright's making, the thing that differentiates it from other writing, is that his "dream-flight," his *improvisation*, has to take into account not only vocal and visual instruments—the actors—but also the peculiar place around which or in front of which he can gather his audience to hear and watch the story—the stage. He is a rare artist because what he puts down on paper, at its most demanding level, is not really writing at all in the usual literary sense, that is, writing intended for consumption in solitude by one person at a time, but is the making of a thing that involves live *actors* and *objects* set out in a specific way for seeing and hearing *by a group* meeting together in a group belonging (the audience). What the play-maker leaves out—the gap for the actors to fill in—is usually as important as what he puts in. French actor-director Jean-Louis Barrault described a play as "interrupted silence." This concept moves us entirely away from thinking about a play as a literary product, as merely conversation written down, for we see it is far more difficult to leave out than to put in. Many celebrated novelists and poets have tried unsuccessfully to make "interrupted silences," but they abandoned their efforts, or audiences forced them to, when they discovered that they didn't have the know-how to devise this sort of skeletal improvisation. Nor did they know what to do with a live audience.

You should not be at all surprised to learn that such famous playwrights as Aeschylus, Shakespeare, and Molière acted in and often directed their own plays. After all, they knew or assumed that they knew, as everybody else did, what their plays were all about. Today, a playwright also hears his words in his mind's ear and sees the actions in his mind's eye when he composes a play. The total thing is the dramatic poem. What the play does to an audience is to arouse its emotions directly. *The process is physical and disturbing,* and it is only *secondarily intellectual,* though the experience requires a perceptive intelligence—not quite the same thing. When it works, it reaches out to grab and thrill; it can cause tears and laughter, chills and anger; it can also exhaust members of an audience as well as exalt them. Its powers are mystical and godlike. As we know, we can retain a well-performed play in our minds for years in the same way that we hold onto an intensively felt personal experience, as characters in plays can seem like exotic friends of many years' acquaintance.

PERCEPTION: PLAY-ANALYSIS

Perception as it is used here simply implies your own personal discovery of what a playscript is all about—your sense and feel of it.

Many people in the theatre shy away from the phrase *play-analysis* because they think it has a dry, academic ring that implies cold, factual, scientific examination of a playscript, a process that will kill their gut (subjective) feelings about it. They assume that good theatre can be made if one *feels* strongly enough about a playscript; good sense and some general backgrounds in theatre will carry one the rest of the way. This book does not agree at all with that point of view. Certainly, there are aspects of many plays that cannot be described easily in words, but this difficulty does not suggest that a play exists in a mystical world defying logical, mind-oriented examination. Having the right attitude about play-analysis at the beginning is very important.

The word *perception* has specific meanings here because it can imply both strong feelings (the subjective flight and freedom in a director) and a basic objective awareness of how a play is made. It implies much more than a felt reaction on a first reading: "I like that play. It moves me strongly." Perception implies that a penetrating search into a play—play analysis—is absolutely necessary if one is to understand how a play works.

What a director finds in his play-analysis will depend on how thoroughly he can take a play apart in his own mind and then put it back together again, thoroughly comprehended. Perception is the director's total view of a playscript after he has "felt" it and then "examined" it in detail. If his feelings are strong on first reading, and he knows the job of play-analysis, he cannot help but have much greater respect for a play after analysis than he had before. At the very least, he will not be ambivalent about it.

This point of view is predicated on the assumption that a play is not life but art form, a made object that may have a likeness to life but definitely is not life. Even those playscripts that seem most realistic, most like everyday life as we know it, stand this test. You may have heard about Stanislavski's discovery of this difference when he asked his actors to perform a scene from a play by Chekhov out-of-doors in a real garden. Before they began, he assumed that the playscript was lifelike and his players so photographically real in their roles that anyone watching could only think what he saw was actually taking place. He was amazed, and at first greatly disappointed, to discover that the scene produced no such effect; against the reality of nature in the garden the action and the actors were like wax flowers with only a resemblance to reality. He then began to revise his whole theory of making reality on the stage, basing it on the realization that a play is a play, no matter how photographic it seems, and must therefore not be confused with real life.

Play-analysis, then, is the director's objective support *for his feelings* about a playscript. As a technique, it is tied to the primary thesis that directing is not a totally intuitive process but is also an art-creating process in which the director brings the materials (the playscript) of the form to the conscious surface; that is, he becomes *consciously* aware of them in the interest of finding their strengths and weaknesses, their peaks and valleys, and their rhythms, all of which will serve as a basis for theatricalizing the playscript in the best possible wa . Adequate play-analysis is no guarantee of success, but it does insure th the director is at least familiar with his materials.

The playscript is the principal machine of the director, and play-analysis is as basic a reason for his job as is helping the actor. Unless he knows his machine thoroughly, he will be only a stage manager—a traffic organizer and logistical expert.

OVERVIEW OF PLAY-ANALYSIS

Study the drawing below very carefully because it is at once a summary of what you will be tangling with not only in Part I on play-analysis but also in Parts II and III as you work at putting a play on stage.

You should note in the drawing the five major areas to examine in taking a play apart: (1) given circumstances, (2) dialogue, (3) dramatic action, (4) characters, and (5) ideas. Two more areas not seen in the drawing will be added to this list: (6) tempos, and (7) moods. Although this breakdown is arbitrary for the purpose of explicit discussion, you should recognize at the outset that they overlap, as the drawing illustrates, and that some of these areas are so thoroughly dependent on others that they do not take shape until the force of the others has been determined. Other words might be used to define the same concepts, but this set, when fully delineated, answers the purpose very well. You know that basic communication in textbooks rests on clear definition of the terms used. Therefore, you must recognize at this point that play-analysis in this book is based on the meanings given to the terms here and in the following three chapters. For the purpose of discussion, the seven areas are treated under three major headings: (1) "The Foundation and Facade of the Playscript: Given Circumstances and Dialogue," discussed in Chapter 3; (2) "The Hard Core of the Playscript: Dramatic Action and Characters," discussed in Chapter 4; and (3) "The Derivatives of Dramatic Action in a Playscript: Idea and Rhythmic Beats," treated in Chapter 5.

You must also be alerted at this point to a matter of great importance: Each of these words (for example, dialogue) or two-word phrases (for example, given circumstances) stands for a concept. Merely to define them is not to understand them. As in acting, *doing* in directing will lie not

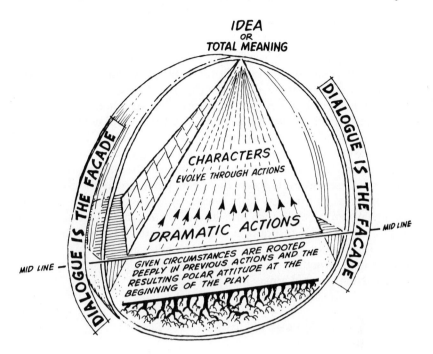

A graphic representation of all playscripts. Note the midline: A play begins here, recapturing the past and moving forward to the present.

in defining terms or in debating concepts but in absorbing them so thoroughly that they are immediately recognizable in all contexts. You must discover for yourself the breadth and depth of these concepts so that they become an intuitive part of your thinking about a play.

In the discussions of the seven areas the terms are first defined and then developed as concepts. Some examples are given to illustrate each step in this technique, but your comprehension will come about only through application of the approach to specific plays. There is no skipping around in this procedure. Try to understand and apply the concept of one term before you go on to the next. The series of seven is developed in an intentional order to show how each draws on what precedes it.

At first, you will be tempted to push aside the examination-in-depth of these concepts. After all, simple impression—"I *feel* it this way"—is much easier. But if you do proceed in this fashion, you will soon discover that you really do not know much about the inside workings of a play and that *you do not really know how to get through to actors*. Once you have mastered the techniques outlined here, you will feel a security you have not known previously, since you will at least know something very specific about your primary tool—the playscript.

Story versus Play-Analysis

Another problem usually confronting the student in his first contacts with play-analysis is the difference between the playscript as mere story and the structure of that story. The story of a play is made up of so many things so well blended together that an unoriented reader merely experiences its final effect: its moods, its feelings. But through play-analysis, the director can get at what makes those moods and feelings. Thus he can have greater assurance of getting the most out of his actors, and in turn, moving audiences. In comparison with live theatre, the moving picture as a form is static because each scene has been perfected through several takes and retakes and is set, impervious to change. In the theatre, however, a playscript is made up of a line of scenes that must be played continuously without interruption, and then repeated at subsequent performances. This living quality is its individuality and its rarity. Your awareness of play structure, then, will give you the seeds for all that can happen later when you put a play into production.

STUDY PLAN FOR PARTS I AND II

Improvisation as a Tool

In this book the technique of *improvisation* is suggested throughout as a classroom work method. In its early uses, improvisation was thought of primarily as Stanislavskian training for the actor, but as its values and possibilities became more apparent, it was used not only in the relationship between director and actor but also as a basis for play-making. Consequently, not only were a number of experimental moving pictures made by using this approach, but the live productions of The Open Theatre and The Living Theatre in the 1960s showed us that unusual theatricals could also be developed through this technique. Though such productions in the 1990s are infrequent, the improvisational approach as a method of freeing both actors and directors in training is still quite valid.

The approach taken in this book, therefore, assumes that stage direction is the process of freeing the master improvisation—the playscript—by freeing actors and designers to make their own improvisations. The imposition of restriction, of limitation, can take place only *after the flight* and not before. One of the great problems in learning directing is in learning this paradox of freedom and restraint. Both are absolutely necessary: Without freedom the imagination of an audience is never aroused; without restraint the telling of the story from the confinement of a stage in a theatre with live actors would be impossible.

The director is therefore an improvisor of the first order. In this sense he is very close to the playwright who turns his dreams into forms—all controlled improvisations. The director is forever a game-player, always improvising, always making up spontaneously what seems appropriate and believable in a given circumstance.

You will note as you work through this book that many of the exercises require improvisation—spontaneous storytelling in declared or undeclared circumstances. If you have participated in such game playing, you will already know that improvising can make something very much like a play, but it is not a play at all, only an exercise in releasing imagination. The overall intention is to free those persons who play the game—to let them "fly." But in order to do so, several conditions are necessary. Here are a few that must guide you and your classmates when doing improvisations:

1. The participants are not actors; that is, they are neither acting out a portion of a playscript nor are they performing for an audience. Their intention is to *release each other* through full concentration on each other and the situation. Although some given circumstances may be set before an improvisation begins, the participants work "off" one another, with their imagination dictating what to do in a certain context. There is no preplan of action. What happens will happen only as a participant lets his behavior, in reaction to other forces (other people in the same improvisation), be the result of his response to their pressures.

2. The watchers are not the audience. They are privileged to be there when the improvisation takes place. Therefore, they must not participate like an audience, but should watch silently and quietly with no verbal reactions whatsoever, since this would break the "happening" by distracting the participants, thus making them self-conscious. Once the participants have become self-aware, the improvisation is lost because they have become themselves and not participants in an imagined circumstance.

3. The place to develop an improvisation is not a stage nor any location that would resemble it, because the artificial nature of this kind of setting would cause the improvisors to feel self-conscious. For this reason this game should be played in a room, with the space defined only by what the improvisors find necessary.

4. Only the beginning of an improvisation should be suggested, and only in a barely minimal way. What happens afterward is the improvisation.

It is obvious that a good deal that is playlike can happen in improvisations if the participants and watchers observe the conditions. You can see characters in action, with different moods and tempos, and, as a watcher, you can be moved by the truth telling and believability of such moments. But you must also realize that "achieving" a complex improvisation is not easily accomplished unless you have participants with experience in playing this game, since learning to release fully takes practice. In working through the exercises in this book you must always give yourself seriously and with full concentration to improvisational exercises. If you do, you will find them most rewarding.

Why Does This Study of Directing Begin with Play-Analysis?

Realism has been the dominant dramaturgical style since Ibsen's day, but it has survived to the present, despite many attempts to pull away, because it is a style that mass audiences can understand and absorb in the technological and psychological climate of the twentieth century. A Realistic play may seem old-fashioned to you. But do not be misled by what you see on the stage in recent productions of plays: multiple scenes and stagings with platforms and fractionated pieces for settings, or even bare stages, and highly selective lighting. They are the outer look. What matters here at the beginning of your study is not how a production looks but your grasp of the underpinnings of all plays—the form—not a specific style like Realism. You must first separate your understanding of *what goes on in a play* (play-analysis) from the staging of that play (production) because you will not be able to stage it with perception and imagination until you do. Otherwise you will be only a stage manager, not a director. Crawl before you try to fly.

It should be sufficient at this point to define *style* as the qualities in a play other than its story that turn the general form into something individual and specific. These unique markings are therefore always present in a play. But you must learn how to take a play apart before you attack the problems of style, the subject of Part III of this book. Realism is a style you can understand more readily because it is the one most familiar to you in what you see actors doing, not only on the stage but also in motion pictures and television drama, for that craft has been rooted in audience communication and not in artful stagings.

Choosing a Class Study Play

A one-act, Realistic play of high quality should be selected by your class, or by the instructor, as a common device for ensuing discussions. A suggestion might be J. M. Synge's familiar classic *Riders to the Sea* because it is so well put together, so well constructed, that it has withstood nearly a century of picking apart while still retaining things to wonder about. It has survived because it is a dramatic poem of true stature and intensive meaning. At first, it may seem simple to you, but you will be looking at the outside not the inside. If you are to understand much about the changes playwrights have made in this century, you must take apart a Realistic play—a play that looks like life around you--and reassemble it fully understood; otherwise you will get lost in disassembling those that are not Realistic. Save those until later.

To offset what may seem old-fashioned about *Riders,* your class may want to look regularly at two other plays, chosen from later periods, to act as "control" plays. One might be a one-act play by Tennessee Williams, written during the 1940s or 1950s, and the other a one-act play by William Albee. But don't let your enthusiasm to direct recent plays kill off what you must learn now about the structure of all plays. Once you understand the principles of play-analysis, and something about Realism, you will be able to disassemble all kinds of plays, including musicals and operas, and make them work for you on the stage. The theatre will wait for you, but it will not want you if you don't know what is going on there.

EXERCISE

A. The Poet and the Director

1. Discuss all the parts of the definitions:
   a. A play is a story brought alive by actors on a stage before an audience.
   b. Plays are musical compositions in dialogue that linger in the memory and are called up with nostalgia like sweet tunes almost forgotten.
   c. Plays move the viewer-listener by plucking the emotional chords that jar loose submerged feelings, and force the turnover of past actions, either happy or unhappy.
2. What is a dramatic poet? Why is a modern writer of drama in prose also a dramatic poet? How does a play differ from a novel or a history?
3. Without getting involved in the complexities of the differences between serious drama and comedy, why is the writer of comedy also a dramatic poet?
4. The director is an "image-maker." What is an image? Cite images of each of the five senses.
5. From your knowledge of acting and designing, can you see how an audience perceives a play through images? What is the process of transfer?

B. Improvisations

1. Illustrate the difference between restriction and flight by doing the following improvisation: With the use of chairs, tables, or other essentially neutral forms in the classroom, one student composes a four-sided place. The class then tries to guess the *literal* place suggested by the forms and their arrangement by identifying the literal meaning of each form, such as a chair, a bed, a sofa, in the context of other forms. When a consensus has been reached on the literal meaning, the class suggests *alternate meanings* for the forms, with the intention of arriving at more exceptional locations and contexts. Thus, what might at first seem to be a normal suburban living room could be turned into the mountain hideout of a gangster or the primitive hut of a peasant. Repeat this game with several

improvised places. The flight takes place as class members move away from accepted literal meanings of forms in their easily recognizable contexts—their own everyday realities—and begin to let the forms take on imagined places. Thus, *forms become the stimulators of flight,* not hard realities. (Note: This exercise is not that of making a groundplan for a stage, so do not set up the places with a stage in mind but only as places that could exist in real life anywhere.)

2. Continue Improvisation Exercise 1 with one student arranging a place and then setting in it two people who have a specific relationship to one another, such as mother/son, boss/secretary, boy/girl. The class tries first to declare the literal place and its context; it then tries to identify possible flights by suggesting more exceptional places and relationships of the people.

3. Continue Improvisation Exercise 2 by having the students in the improvisation *develop a conflict* by using numbers, not words, as dialogue. Example: *A* says: 1, 2, 3, 4; *B* says: 9, 10, 20; *A* says: 2, 3, 6, 7; *B* says: 4, 7, 9, 10. In this substitute for dialogue, the numbers do not mean anything in themselves, but the attitude behind each group of numbers is the basic meaning behind the line. (The use of actual words in improvisations is very difficult for participants because they must think in terms of word choice. Number dialogue is much easier because participants need think only of their attitudes towards other people in the improvisation.) When the improvisers reach an intensity of interresponse, the improvisation can be stopped and the following points discussed:
   a. What is improvisation?
   b. What are the free circumstances of an improvisation?
   c. How was this improvisation like a play and yet not a play?
   d. What is a play? (Try defining it as an expert and highly developed improvisation.)
   e. What did the participants add to the suggested beginning of the improvisation?
   f. What are the limitations in the use of number dialogue?

PART ONE

TAKING A PLAY APART
Play-Analysis: The Director's Primary Study

Ingrid Bergman on Alfred Hitchcock:

He is a magnificently prepared director.
There is nothing that he does not know about
the picture he is going to do. Every angle
and every set-up he has prepared at home. . . .
He does not even look into the camera, for he
says, "I know what it looks like."

Ingria Bergman, *My Story*

Chapter Three

THE FOUNDATION AND FACADE OF THE PLAYSCRIPT
Given Circumstances and Dialogue

After you have read the following pages you will have a better understanding of why "Foundation and Facade" has been chosen to head this chapter. All you need to understand at this point, however, is that both given circumstances and dialogue *frame* the play just as deeply rooted pilings and a covering of glass and steel frame a modern skyscraper. The given circumstances resemble the deeply rooted base of a building—the substructure upon which it is built, its foundation; and dialogue is the outer shell, the facade, the transparent encasement covering the activities that will go on inside. If you keep these images in mind, you will be able to see why the real guts of the play (its hard core) resides in dramatic action and characters, but that they cannot be built into the structure without the foundation of given circumstances and the facade of dialogue.

GIVEN CIRCUMSTANCES (PLAYWRIGHT'S SETTING): THE FOUNDATION

Definition

The term *given circumstances* (playwright's setting) concerns all material in a playscript that delineates the environment—the special "world" of the play—in which the action takes place. This material includes: (1) environmental facts (the specific conditions, place, and time); (2) previous action (all that has happened before the action begins); and (3) polar attitudes (points of view toward their environment held by the principal characters).

Given Circumstances versus Playwright's Setting

Although Stanislavski's phrase "given circumstances" will be used throughout this text after this initial explanation, the parenthetical phrase *playwright's setting* is used because you are probably more familiar with it. However, as a term, it is so frequently confused with what a designer makes—the actual stage construction—that you should avoid using it altogether. Many readers of plays, including students of the theatre early in their training, commonly assume that the explicit directions describing a room or other location that usually appear in the printed editions of modern plays have been set down by their authors. However, more often than not, they depict the settings used in the first production and thus represent the conception of the designers as recorded by a stagemanager or an editor. Even when such a description comes from an author's own manuscript, a further danger exists because the author may try to play the role of stage designer, a role about which he may know little or nothing at all. If you, as a reader-director, are not aware of this pitfall, you may find it very difficult to free yourself from these initial suggestions because the printed word may seduce you. There is much less harm in reading these directions after you have studied the play, for then you will have a strong conception of the inherent setting, and you can separate what the author considers significant about an environment from a designer's interpretation of it.

Dialogue is the only reliable source of given circumstances.   When you study plays, you quickly become aware that all authors write their settings directly into their dialogue, either overtly or subconsciously. Given circumstances are a matter of feeling about objects and places, about time and what has happened before the play begins, and about the feelings of the characters for the special world of the play. The totality is what a playwright must communicate to the audience as deftly and as accurately as possible, for what happens in a play will be based on these given circumstances.

Analyzing the Given Circumstances

You will note in the suggested analytical technique that follows that the first two sections—"Environmental Facts" and "Previous Action"—are far more factual than the third—"Polar Attitudes." Yet it is this last that will actually set up the beginning point of a play because it is the most important aspect of the given circumstances. Look for the facts, yes; but the attitudes of characters toward those facts are extremely important.

Environmental facts.   All plays establish some delineation of the exact place and time of the action as well as give specific information about the environment. These elements are called the facts of the play *whether or not the playwright has been historically accurate,* because they remain fixed throughout the play. The director should isolate them by systematically noting them under the following categories:

1. Geographical location—the exact place. This category should also include climate, since weather often defines specific location and can affect dramatic action.
2. Date—year, season, time of day. What is significant about the date?
3. Economic environment—class level, state of wealth or poverty. If two or more economic levels are used in a play, be certain to record the facts of each level.
4. Political environment—the specific relationships of the characters to the form of government under which they live. Many plays have definite political settings that will strongly affect the behavior of the characters. Many other plays tacitly accept a form of government that has established basic restrictions on the characters. Do not take what you may think is direct omission to mean that it is unimportant. Look carefully for clues throughout the script, for the author may be taking this given circumstance for granted on the assumption that those who read the play will understand the context. But *you* cannot make such an assumption. He will leave a trail of implications behind him, and these you must dig out.
5. Social environment—the mores and social institutions under which the characters live. These facts are extremely important because they may be manifested through their restrictions on the outward behavioral patterns of the characters and consequently may set up basic conflicts in the action of the play.
6. Religious environment—formal and informal psychological controls. Much that applies to item 4 also applies here.

When you study the given circumstances of a play, you must strictly avoid reading anything into the play; all facts must be explicitly stated or implied as is suggested in item 4 of the list. Do not assume anything. Some plays will involve all of these categories; others only some of them. Above all, *do not try to reconstruct your own idea of historical fact* surrounding a play; *if it is not in the play, it does not exist.* A playwright is not writing a history but telling a story; and he may not know his history well at all, or he may be deliberately shifting the facts to suit his own purposes. Do not try to correct him but record his facts exactly as he prescribes them.

Previous action.   It is necessary to make a sharp distinction between *present action*—what an audience actually sees *happening* immediately in front of it—and *previous action*—what an audience is *told happened before the present action begins.* All plays begin somewhere in the middle or toward the end of things; thus, given circumstances usually includes some *narration* of past action so that the present action has a base from which to move forward. More recent plays, those written since the early 1960s, depend very little on past action, whereas others, those of Ibsen, for instance, require much retelling of past events. Both kinds of action—previous and present—are included in what is loosely defined as a story. But the director *always works specifically with present action*, although one of his major problems is to decide how to make the necessary narrations about the past as active as possible. In modern plays based on psychological revelation, the past plays an enormous part in the explanation as it does in a Freudian psychoanalysis; yet, the vital play for audiences lies only in what is actively happening immediately before its eyes.

You must, therefore, learn to separate these two kinds of action. The previous action, though it may take all of the first act and sometimes longer to narrate fully, establishes the point where the present action actually begins. Once you learn how to make this distinction you will know how to make a narration of the past interesting on the stage, for narration in itself is very dull compared to present action. Yet, a good playwright will always make this narration exciting because he will give the character a present action in the process of recalling it; that is, he will arrange for the recounting to do something to a character we are watching. Thus, to the director, *there is never a dull exposition but only a recalling of the past under the excitement and tension of active engagement with other characters in the present.* A director who does not know this point of structure will lose control of his audience very quickly. He will lose the key to handling the plays of Ibsen and Chekhov as well as a great deal of twentieth-century drama.

A technique for separating these two areas of action is the simple one of underlining in the text all lines that *recall* the past. A text by Ibsen contains many such lines, particularly in the first act; and often there are important revelations later in the play, especially when new characters are introduced. If you list these previous actions on one-half of a sheet of paper as they are introduced and put down the present actions, you will see their direct relationship.

A director can obscure a production by careless inattention to previous action, for some playwrights handle the necessary recalling in such subtle ways that an audience will miss important points unless the director carefully sets them out. Plays do not "talk" themselves; they are communicated by actors and directors who know what they are "talking" about. Congreve's *The Way of the World* is a great play, one of the greatest in the English language; but if an audience misses the point, made very briefly in one line, that Mirabell was once a lover to Mrs. Fainall, that he left her pregnant, and that he arranged for her marriage to Fainall, the import of most of the action that follows involving Mirabell as well as Fainall will be misunderstood and its significance lost. This example is extreme, but in kind it is forever recurring.

Learn what previous action is and then you will know what to do with it in production.

Polar attitudes. Every character in a play, as in real life, is conditioned by the "special world" he is caught in, the world of his own prejudices, his own tolerances and intolerances, and his assumptions when he is forced to have relationships with others and must take actions affecting both himself and others. The special world of a character is conditioned, of course, by environmental facts and by previous action. Although it depends on these concrete details, it differs explicitly in that it is the "emotional environment" of a character, the stresses and strains under which he lives. Modern slang would call them his "hang-ups." The special world of the principal character is always declared *at the beginning of a play* because it declares his position vis-à-vis the other characters. This is the *inner environment* of a play, the environment that sets up the conflicts and the problems: the environment of love relationships in and out of marriage; the environment of family pressures that cause love and hate between mothers and sons, fathers and sons, mothers and daughters; the environment of political, religious, and social pressures that force people to behave in ways that may destroy their families and their relationships to these families; the environments of fear of power, disregard of others, indifference to wealth or love of wealth, indifference to religion or its opposite. A character is caught in this special world, and the play is about how he is destroyed by it or escapes from it.

Here is an important fact about plays: In the course of a play a *principal* character *does not change* in character, but his *attitudes change* under pressures from forces outside his control. The other characters serve as specific instruments to these changes. As the principal character meets these forces, he must adjust to them, and, as he does so, certain capabilities dormant within him (his true character) come to the surface and force him to act. These capabilities have been present all the time, but they have never been called upon and thus recognized as points of character. The development in a play's action, therefore, is composed of the changing attitudes in the principal character towards his *inner* environment, towards *his special world* as it was declared at the beginning of the play.

It is also important to point out that all of the characters in a play do not change their attitudes, but only the principal characters, a fact that makes them principal. Secondary characters thus act as instruments in these changes. In a play-analysis it is always the primary characters that concerns us most, for then we can determine the exact force and functions of the secondary characters.

Most plays show radical shifts in the attitudes of their principal characters from the positions they held at the beginning to those they hold at the end. A philosophical way of expressing this shift is to say that a character moves from ignorance to knowledge. He sees the world in which he lives more and more clearly *after* the actions he has been forced to take during the course of the play than he did before. Therefore, it is necessary to pin down the attitudes towards the inner environment (special world) held at the beginning of a play by a principal character so that a director can clearly see the final pole of his character, and can later help the actor find both poles, as well as help the other characters see their function in the change. What happens in between these poles is the dramatic action.

By setting out the polar attitudes of each principal character, the director can see the scope of what happens in between the poles—the stretch of the characters—and the explicit effects given circumstances have on the characters. Thus, the shape of the play is explicitly declared in the polarities of the principal character.

What we mean by the beginning of a play, then, is the defined positions of the attitudes held by the principal character of the play toward the special world he is caught in and within which he takes action. These positions declare explicitly where the *present action* begins. The characters in most plays (Ionesco's antihero is an exception) will have strong feelings of either like or dislike for the present inner environment in which they find themselves. The plot that follows (present action) will either shake them loose from their liking or bring their dislike to liking (or at least to acceptance). If a character does not finally accept what he dislikes at the beginning of a play, he will probably die or exile himself in the process of resisting the forced change that others bring upon him and become what we call a *tragic hero*. In comedy, if a character strongly resists being pried loose from what he already likes intensely at the beginning, he will survive, but he will be ridiculed and become what we call a *comic fool*. But whatever happens to him, the attitudes he has at the beginning will certainly be radically changed by the end, or if he is a certain kind of comic fool, he may go on blissfully, never realizing that anyone has tried to change him. (See Exercise 5 at the end of this section.)

An attitude towards the special world at the beginning of a play is usually more general than specific. It is usually something the character has taken for granted as the natural state of affairs, and he is therefore not consciously aware of it, although it most certainly will be pointed out to the audience in one way or another. The action of the play will make him aware of his special world because it will subject him to a test of his attitudes through direct conflict with others. The initial action in a play will usually point out to him where he stands in contrast to others, although he may be very blind about why he stands where he does. The attitudes of characters, then, should be general statements and not tied specifically to the present action which will follow. Here are some examples of initial attitudes:

> Men are foolish and romantic and can be manipulated rather easily. (Hedda in *Hedda Gabler*. What is her final attitude?)
>
> The only thing that really matters is money. (Regina in *The Little Foxes*. What is her final attitude?)
>
> "Good" women are dull, embarrassing, and impossible to talk to. (Marlowe in *She Stoops to Conquer*. What is his final attitude?)
>
> A king is sacred and no one can challenge his God-given right to dictate. (Oedipus in *Oedipus Rex*. What is his final attitude?)
>
> Love of women is all romantic adoration and worship. (Marchbanks in *Candida*. What is his final attitude?)

When you have learned to pinpoint the special world of a play, you will understand the secret of its inner workings because you will know what the environmental forces are that hold the principal characters in check at the beginning. This knowledge will show you what they must fight against to overcome those forces in order to arrive at the final pole.

In the actual practice of trying to determine polar attitudes, it is usually easier to find the initial pole for each character by noting what has happened to each character at the end. Remember that the interest of an audience will be focused on what happens between the poles, for this is the dramatic action, the specifics that bring about the change in the principal characters. This is what holds the audience so riveted to the play and what makes the change so climactic, so theatrical, and so emotionally disturbing.

Significance of the environmental facts. A final step of great importance in your analysis is determining how the environmental facts affect the total meaning of a play. The best way to do this is to make a strong summary statement that points this out. Environmental facts often drive the action directly, as Ibsen and Strindberg demonstrated in their plays, a technique that set the style of Realism and the plays that followed in this mode. The clash in class differences is frequently among the strongest generators of action. Tennessee Williams's *A Streetcar Named Desire*, for instance, takes place in the French Quarter of New Orleans, a fact that intensifies Blanche's already precarious emotional condition. In this instance, the location functions almost as a character by bombarding Blanche with tastes and smells; horrible sights and sounds; and gritty, slimy, filthy surfaces; and by defeating her intention of finding sanctuary in her sister, Stella. She also has no privacy and is subjected to the nightly sounds of her hosts' wild lovemaking. When Stanley rapes Blanche and drives her into insanity, Williams uses the actions in that environment as a metaphor for the backward slide of civilization versus the gentility of the

Old South. He is thus able to use the *environment in action* to make his point.

EXERCISE

1. Using any modern Realistic play (*Riders to the Sea, Ghosts, Hedda Gabler, Desire Under the Elms*), list the environmental facts in the specific categories suggested in this chapter. What do these facts suggest about a possible stage setting? Can you "see" the setting? Can you visualize some possible costumes? What do they tell you about body movement? About decorum? Do they suggest what the characters think about and what they feel? What does physical circumstance (environmental fact) have to do with human behavior? (Begin the cumulative analysis of your class study play at this point. See p. 14.)
2. Delineate the previous action in the same play you have studied in Exercise 1 by underlining all the parts of the speeches in the first act that literally refer to actions that have happened *before* the here-and-now of the act begins. If you are looking at *Hedda Gabler* or another play by Ibsen, how many lines by actual count contain references to previous actions? (Be very careful not to include those recountings of actions that the audience has already witnessed as present actions; those narrations are present actions because the playwright intends the audience to weigh and evaluate a character in terms of that character's judgments of what has happened.) In your own judgment, what is the effect of this accumulation of knowledge about the past? Does it have any effect on what is happening in the present? Does it tell us anything about the characters? Can you see why it is unimportant in itself, but only as it affects a character's present action?
3. *Very important:* As an alternate exercise, study several opening pages of a play by listing the previous action on one side of a sheet and the present action on the other. In this way you have a ready comparison of what the playwright is actually doing.
4. In working with the same play used in Exercises 1 through 3, delineate the attitude of each major character toward the special world or the inner emotional environment of the play—what he thinks and feels about life around him. Whether he likes it or not is unimportant; what he likes about it or does not like about it is very important. Look for such hidden attitudes as: love for others, fear of power, disregard of others, indifference to wealth, indifference to religious feeling. Does he admire monarchy? Does he love freedom? Let the emotional environment tell you exactly how each major character reacts to the given world at the beginning of the play.
5. Discuss Archie Bunker's polar attitudes in reruns of television's *All in the Family*. Do you see how he changes during the course of an episode (comparable to a one-act play)? What is the function of "Meathead"? Of Archie's wife and daughter?

DIALOGUE: THE FACADE OF THE PLAYSCRIPT

Now that you understand the roots of a play—where, when, and how it derives from the immediate past (the given circumstances)—you are ready to examine its facade: the clothes on the package. What is inside will be given special attention in Chapter 4 when you study dramatic action and characters. But now you need to become aware that dialogue is not just the things people say but also, far more importantly, *what they do.*

Definition

Although dialogue is obviously the conversation between *two or more* characters in a play, it is not so obvious that *its primary function is to "contain" the dramatic action,* to be its primary vehicle. In addition, although dialogue may appear as a written line on a printed page, its primary intention is to be *heard* rather than read. It is talk and not writing.

Dialogue Is Action

Dialogue is not merely a verbal interchange between characters but an artificial, highly economical, and symbolic intercommunication of *actions* between characters in which each forces his wants and needs on the other. *Dialogue always exists in the present tense* because it comes out of the mouths of speakers who think, as in life, only in the present and who say things to one another to get what they want.

Dialogue Is a Building Process

A says something to *B,* and *B* replies; this talk causes *A* to reply to *B* and *B* to *A* in a continuing cycle. But no matter how refined a line of dialogue may be, no matter how elaborate the choice of words, the purpose is always the same: to seek response out of another person as we do in real life.

Thus, the nature of dialogue is its built-in characteristic of *"forcing."* The words used on the outside may try to conceal this forcing in a very elaborate way, or they may be very direct and not conceal it at all. From a casual reader's view, dialogue looks like it is only the printed text of the play, but its basic function is to contain the heart and soul, the blood and guts of the play—*the subtext* or dramatic action.

Dialogue Is in Verse or Prose

Plays vary greatly in the choice of language used by characters, a choice that the given circumstances dictate since they specifically delineate the decorum or outward show, that is, how the characters behave—their manners or lack of manners. Most modern plays have prose dialogue because of its likeness to the reality of everyday life; but a few are written in verse forms as were many plays of the past. Verse forms are obviously more artificial in their use of language than is prose, but the basic intent is always the same: the containment of the dramatic action. More will be said about verse later in Part III in the discussion of plays of past ages, but it is sufficient to point out here that verse form is not merely a decorative exterior but a heightened, more compact, exalting language for conveying intense feelings and high actions. The effect of verse is often as potent as physical body movements, simply because verse conveys intensive inner feelings at the highest pitch. It thus has the capability of direct contact with an audience. This is why many playwrights who write dialogue in prose often try to find a language somewhat more elevated than what is used in everyday life, as Arthur Miller did in *The Crucible*.

Dialogue Is Inner Language

Dialogue should be analyzed in detail to discover its peculiar characteristics in addition to its function as a cover for dramatic action and its direct reflection of given circumstances. Even within the narrow range of the given circumstances for a particular play, an author has a large scope in his choice of words and their arrangement and in the images he may devise. Dialogue is thus said to be *connotative* rather than denotative— much more weighted with feeling and meaning than dictionary usage or definitive meaning. In the human context of plays, characters feel or sense one another (as people who live closely together do in everyday life) and consequently do not talk at one another but *with* one another. Thus, the language of drama is highly subjective, inner language. Realism has used a wide variety of folk-speech patterns—dialects—in the interest of showing how people talk from their "guts" and not from their minds. Moving pictures have fully exploited this aspect of dialogue, particularly in reproducing low-level environments.

Dialogue Is Heard Language

Any study of a play written in dialect requires penetration beyond the choice of words and the modification of vowels, for an author who has really heard the speech he uses for a certain character will reproduce all sorts of cultural overtones buried in the outer form, a subtle delineation of given circumstances. Thus, the speech sounds of Brooklyn or Dublin or London reflect the hardness of city life, just as Southern American speech reflects the slower rhythm of the rural South. Most recent plays that intend reproduction of local idiom (August Wilson's plays, for instance) do not set down the modifications of sound in spelling as playwrights once did, but rely on the specific choice of words or lack of them to convey the inarticulate aspects of the characters. The dialect (sound quality) is thus left to the actor to supply.

Directors must, therefore, learn to hear dialogue in their mind's ear: not only the literal reproductions of sound as they hear it in everyday life, but the reproduction of word-feeling as playwrights set them out in characters. You must learn the craft of matching speech decorum, as perceived in a play's text from the given circumstances, to character decorum. More will be said about this technique later in connection with acting and actors. (See Exercise 2 in this chapter.)

Dialogue Is Structured of Lines and Speeches

As has already been pointed out, dialogue is artificially contrived. A close examination of any good play will show that the author has usually arranged his sentence structure to throw the important phrase—the actual point of each line—to the end of the line. This placement makes it climactic. Speeches made up of several sentences are carefully constructed in the same way. When a director is aware of this technique, he can be more certain of getting good line readings from his actors, and he will be more able to accomplish the desirable emphasis that he knows the play requires throughout.

The director's knowledge of line and speech structure can be aided greatly by the study of what is labeled "Interpretation" or "Interpretive Reading" in university curriculums. In that study, the attention is concentrated on word and line values. At its base is the study of grammar, for grammar is the basis of effective speech, although no one actually thinks of grammar in carrying on a conversation. No director can go very far with actors, however, without a full awareness of word forms and punctuation, and their distinctive uses in the interlocking arrangements that comprise sentence structure. Many directors and actors trained in Stanislavskian approaches assume that if the subtext of a line is fully comprehended, the technical delivery of that line is assured. This assumption is simply not true, for the subtext and the text must both be communicated. This double value will be discussed in detail in Chapter 15 on the oral delivery of the text, but the important thing to understand here is that the *basis* for all dramatic meaning is the subtext—the inner quality of the line. This will be discussed in detail under "Characteristics of Dramatic Action" in the next chapter.

EXERCISE

1. Read aloud some dialogue from *Riders to the Sea,* or another study play, and attempt to reproduce the lines according to the word order and other

speech modifications. What does it sound like? Can you get in the swing of it? Now play a phonograph recording of an actor speaking in a dialect. (Dublin slum-Irish or New York's Brooklynese will do). Why does it sound more genuine than your attempts? Can you pick out any national characteristics in the sound alone? Can you hear social and economic circumstances? Can you hear the specific character traits in the sound?

2. Apply the same test to reruns of the television sit-com *Taxi*. Can you visualize a "plain" script without the detailed inflections used by the actors? Why are the dialects so important to the dramatic action?

3. Examine some prose dialogue from a play by O'Neill. Point out the specific characteristics in the choice of words, the length of sentences and speeches, and the climactic build in each speech. Is the important word or phrase at the end? Does he seem to repeat any particular group of "sense" words? What does O'Neill's dialogue sound like when spoken? Try it.

4. Have two actors read aloud from a play by Harold Pinter. Examine in detail Pinter's development of a particular line, and then of a group of lines. Do you hear given circumstances in the lines? What do you sense about the characters, about how inarticulate they are? What sort of dialects does Pinter intend?

5. Read aloud a passage from Maxwell Anderson's *Winterset*. Can you hear his regular beat, his verse form? What does the verse form do that prose would not do? Repeat the same experiment with T. S. Eliot's *Murder in the Cathedral*. Can you hear his different verse forms? Can you identify their beats (number of stresses in each line)? What does his word choice and verse form add that prose could not accomplish? For contrast, read aloud a passage from Eliot's *The Cocktail Party,* which he wrote in a verse form, although he declared that it ought to sound like prose.

Note: Exercise in the dramatic-action characteristics of dialogue is delayed until after the explanation of dramatic action in the next section.

Chapter Four

THE HARD CORE
OF THE PLAYSCRIPT
Dramatic Action
and Characters

Dramatic action is the clash of forces in a play—the continuous conflict between characters. Here lies the emotional content that moves audiences. Understanding the action will unlock the play because drama means *doing* or *acting*. The hard core of all plays is thus action and characters—the instruments that effect the action or are affected by it and forced to take action of their own.

Dramatic action and the characters are thus inextricably tied together, a fact of dramatic form that you will understand better as you work through the contents of this chapter. The word *plot* is used here in the way playwrights or literary critics use it to describe the sequential arrangement of the conflict incidents that compose the action. For the purposes of detailed discussion in this chapter, dramatic action and characters are treated separately so that you can see their individual characteristics more clearly in isolation.

Understanding the nature and mechanics of dramatic action is a primary study of the director because action is the lifeforce of a play, and because it is the living blood and viscera out of which all other forces grow. Unless the director comprehends its workings, he cannot possibly command the play in directing the actors or in effecting the physical production. He will always be guessing. Again, what happens in a play is the action; it is what holds an audience, thrills them, or makes them laugh.

Unless the student of directing understands the concept of action, unless he pursues it avidly to the core, he will not master the basic tool of his trade. Once he has discovered what action is and how it works in various plays, all the other worlds of play production will open up to him.

As has already been pointed out, plays are not realities but artificial devices—contrivances, if you will—that may be likened, through analogy, to a human body. Just as the heart and other vital organs make possible living and breathing in the human being, so dramatic action provides the same lifegiving force to the play.

Since a play is a work of art, it can be examined and taken apart. Thus, a student who fails to study a play's action is proceeding only on the tenuous grounds of his feelings. His job is to find out not what he feels about a play but what the author, the first improvisor, has put into his playscript. The hard-core study in play-analysis is understanding the action.

CHARACTERISTICS OF DRAMATIC ACTION

Present Tense

As has already been noted in the discussion on dialogue, dramatic action exists only in the present tense. Thus, the participants in the action—the characters—are always in a state of "I do," not "I did." This is what gives the living quality to a play and what makes us aware that it is occurring here and now. Whenever two people meet in a play, as in real life, they start "doing" to each other, and this is what we watch through a time sequence. A play turns on life, and we watch and hear it being lived in front of us. There is never any past tense during a play's life; everything that happens, even the ways the previous action is conveyed, must occur in the present.

Dramatic Action Is Not Activity

It is important at the outset of this discussion to understand the difference between dramatic action and an actor's activity. The latter is the *illustration* of the action: what one actor or one director may have decided best shows the action. Such illustrations or pieces of business—sitting in a chair, crossing the stage, gesturing with the hand, etc.—can be infinite, but the basic dramatic action is fixed within a narrow range. *Acting is, therefore, the process of illustrating the dramatic action—through activity. Activity is the how; action is the what.*

It is necessary to point out these distinctions, because the nineteenth-century common stage tradition usually accepted by actors and stage managers held that illustrations or pieces of business performed by actors were the actions themselves, a tradition still surviving in opera. This misconception of action has unfortunately been carried over into some theatre training with the result of placing a director's attention on superficialities rather than on basic drives and forces in a play. Understanding Realistic plays as well as knowing how to exploit the methods of the modern actor both require uncovering the dramatic action, for only then can the search for appropriate illustrations to externalize it take place. *Activities are thus the externalization of dramatic action.*

All Action Is Reciprocal

As defined previously, action is the clash of forces, the forces being the characters. All action, therefore, forces counteraction, or action in two directions with adjustments in between. The cycle goes this way: (1) *A* does to *B*; (2) *B* feels the force of *A*'s action (adjustment) and decides what action to take; (3) *B* does to *A*; (4) *A* feels the force of *B*'s action (adjustment) and decides what action to take. This cycle is then ready to begin again, but this time on a new and different level. This reciprocal process is carried on until either (1) *A* or *B* is destroyed; or (2) some outside force interrupts the progression (another character enters); or (3) the playwright arbitrarily concludes the action (end of scene).

All dramatic action is therefore *reciprocal;* there is no one-way road but always a *returned* action. Forcing goes on in both directions. Note that *a very important part of this cycle lies in the adjustment* that each character must make before taking a new action. As a result, much of the acting an actor does lies in receiving the force of the other character's action and in deciding what action to take himself. This not only excites the audience but moves the scene continuously forward.

The forcing or the doing, however, can take place in so many gradations that it frequently *looks* as if one character were dominating the other so strongly that the scene gives the appearance of one-way action. But this appearance is all a matter of quiet, low-key adjustment, as is the timing of the adjustment; the action will shift in the other direction before long, and the dominated becomes the dominator. Scenes in plays are composed of *A*'s dominance with *B* taking retreating actions; then *B* takes over and dominates *A*, who takes retreating action. The climax of the scene is reached when either *A* or *B* successfully dominates the other completely. But there is always another possible encounter, for a play is made up of delayed adjustments and the new actions they foment. Sooner or later the dominated one will have another chance, with the possibility that he will emerge as the dominant force. A play moves forward, and the audience continues to be interested, just as long as *A* and *B* are in conflict over who will dominate. Once this question has been answered satisfactorily, a state of relative calm prevails, and the play is concluded.

But unless both characters (forces) are destroyed, the end of one play may only set up the given circumstances for the beginning of another one.